THEORY

Activity Book 1

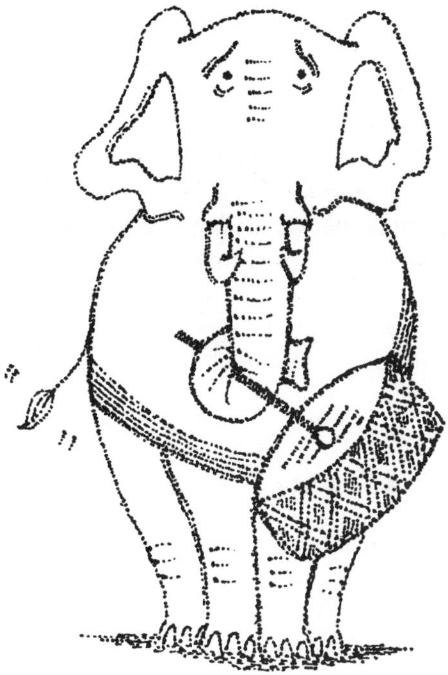

Maureen Cox

First published 1998
by **Subject Publications**

Third impression 2006

ISBN 1 898771 12 X

★ ★ ★ ★ ★ ★

Cover Illustration by Emma Nicholson

Printed by Pardy & Son (Printers) Ltd.,
Parkside, Ringwood, Hampshire, BH24 3SF
Tel: +44 (0)1425 471433
Fax: +44 (0)1425 478923

For Madison

★ ★ ★ ★ ★ ★

Acknowledgements

I am grateful to the many Professional Private Music Teachers who use *Theory is Fun* with their pupils and who have encouraged me to produce this book of activities. I should especially like to thank Melanie Fuller, Stewart Green, Olivia Gribble, Brenda Harris, Judith Homes, Alison Hounsome, Ann Leggett and Marion Martin for their very constructive comments and helpful suggestions.

Maureen Cox

★ ★ ★ ★ ★ ★

This book may be used for extra work and revision of the topics in Theory Is Fun Grade 1.

Complete these pages in Theory is Fun Grade 1 ↓	before tackling the following pages in this activity book. ↓
1 - 21 inc.	6
1 - 23 inc.	7 - 9
1 - 25 inc.	10 - 11
1 - 27 inc.	12 - 15
1 - 35 inc.	16
1 - 37 inc.	17
1 - 42 inc.	18 - 19
1 - 49 inc.	20
1 - 55 inc.	21 - 22
1 - 58 inc.	23
1 - 67 inc.	24 - 25
1 - 69 inc.	26

CONTENTS

Match the Letters and Notes

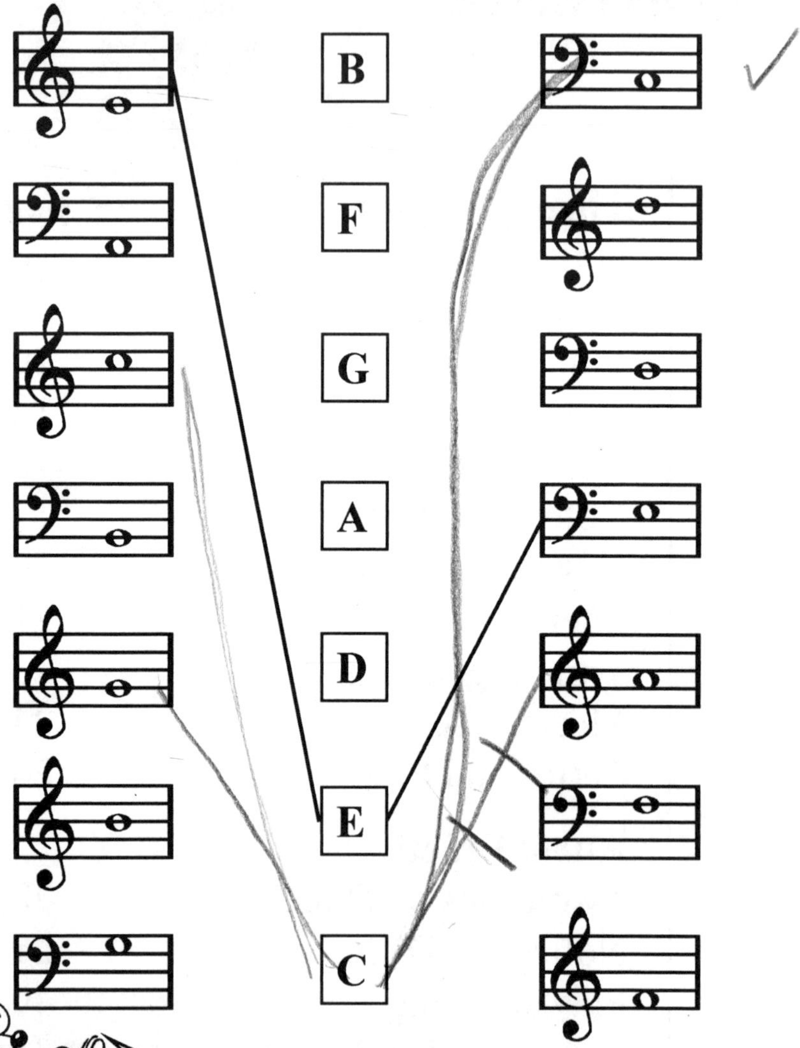

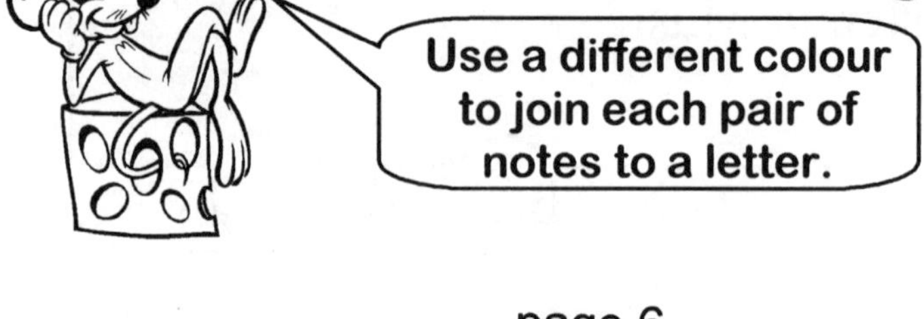

/14

Multiple Choice 1

Tick ☑ the correct note

1. 

D ☐ F ☐ B ☐

2. 

G ☐ E ☐ B ☐

3. 

D ☐ F ☐ G ☐

4. 

A ☐ C ☐ E ☐

5. 

A ☐ F ☐ D ☐

6. 

F ☐ G ☐ B ☐

7. 

F ☐ G ☐ D ☐

8. 

F ☐ G ☐ B ☐

9. 

E ☐ C ☐ A ☐

10. 

E ☐ C ☐ A ☐

/10

A Happy Ending

On a far-off planet there

lived an  egg -shaped creature.

Each day he rolled out of  bed

at seven o'clock, looked at his  _ _ _ _

in the mirror and  _ _ _ _ _ _ _ _ his eyes.

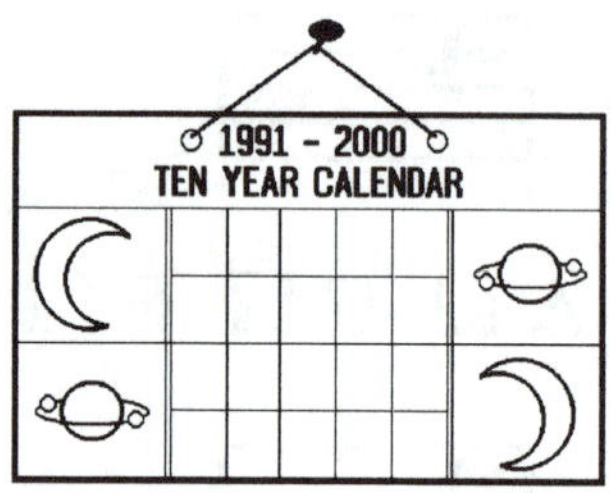

He had been alone

for a 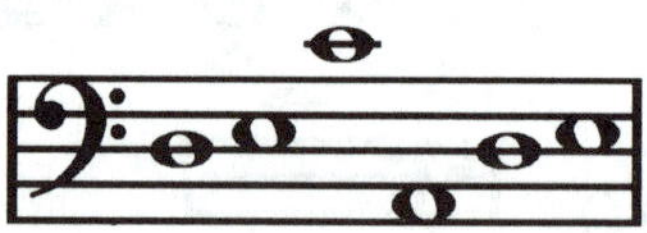 _ _ _ _ _ _ _ _ (ten years).

Then suddenly, at the 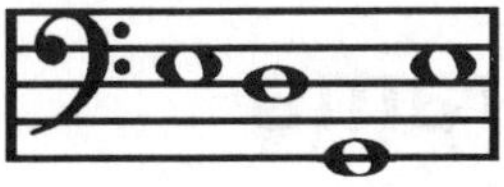 _ _ _ _ of the

planet, he saw a space ship. 

His  _ _ _ had come back for him

because he was old enough to travel.

He rolled into the space ship and smiled

as the far-off planet  _ _ _ _ _ _

out of sight.

Anagrams

Unjumble	Join	Write the word
bleert flec	♩	
threctoc	♪	
sabs flec	𝄞	
mesiravequ	𝅘𝅥𝅯	
mesireveb	𝅗𝅥	minim
ravequ	𝄢	
nimim	𝅝	

/ 7

Discover the Notes

Unjumble the letters on each face to find a note. Write the name of the note under the correct face. Draw the note in the box.

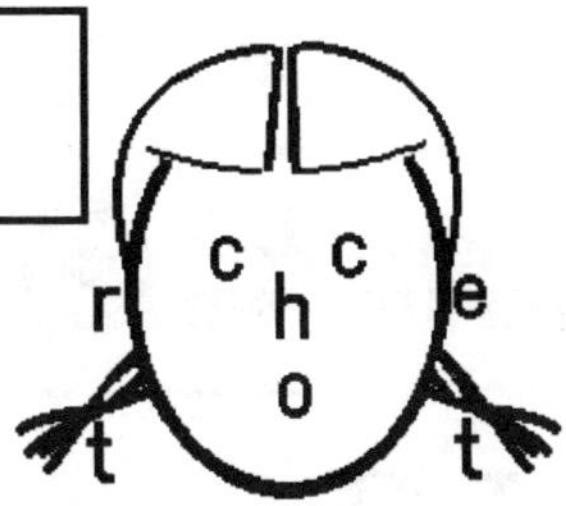

_ _ _ _ _ _ _ _ _ _ _ _ _ _ _

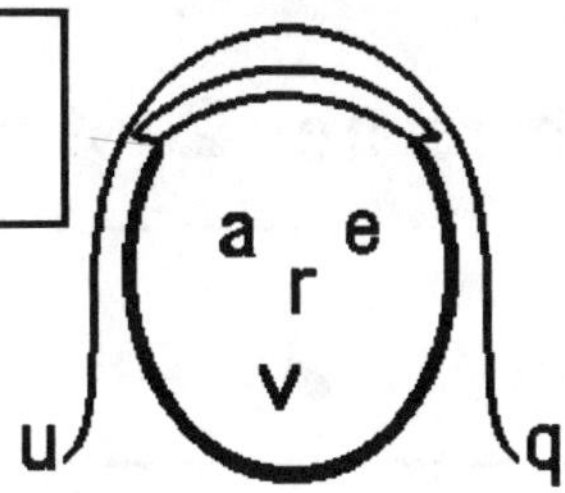

_ _ _ _ _ _ _ _ _ _ _ _ _ _ _ _ _

4

The Minim and the Crotchet

A **rebus** is a puzzle with pictures instead of words. Read this story and write the missing words underneath the pictures.

1 day a  met a  .

_ _ _   _ _ _ _ _ _   _ _ _ _ _ _ _ _ _ _

 am ~~**p**~~ **b**  and you are ~~**b**~~ **sm**  ,

_   _ _ _   _ _ _ _ _ _

boasted the  . **T**  is true,

_ _ _ _ _ _   _ _ _ _

but **W**  we play 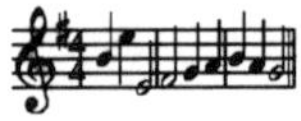 together

_ _ _ _   _ _ _ _ _ _

there are **2** of me ~~**K**~~  **1** of you, said

_ _ _   _ _ _   _ _ _

the  . Let us  ~~**e**~~ friends.

_ _ _ _ _ _ _ _ _   _ _

After that day they played together all the

 . The  never **b** ~~**t**~~  ~~**k**~~ **d** again.

_ _ _ _   _ _ _ _ _   _ _ _ _ _ _ _ _

Jumbled Notes

1. Colour the white letters.

S E M A I M

I M U O N T

Sort the coloured letters to spell a note.

_ _ _ _ _ Now draw it here. →

How many quavers are there in this note? ___

2. Colour the white letters.

B R O T S C V

C U E V T H M

Sort the coloured letters to spell a note.

_ _ _ _ _ _ _ _ Draw it.

How many semiquavers are in this note? ___

4

An Animal Puzzle

Find the first letter of each animal. Write them **in any order**. _ _ _ _ _ _ _ _ _ _ _

Sort out the letters for the **name of a note**.

_ _ _ _ _ _ _ _ _ _ _ Draw the note.

A MUSICAL CROSSWORD

Use the clues to
fit in these words:

SEMIQUAVER	**QUAVER**
SEMIBREVE	**MINIM**
CROTCHET	**CLEFS**

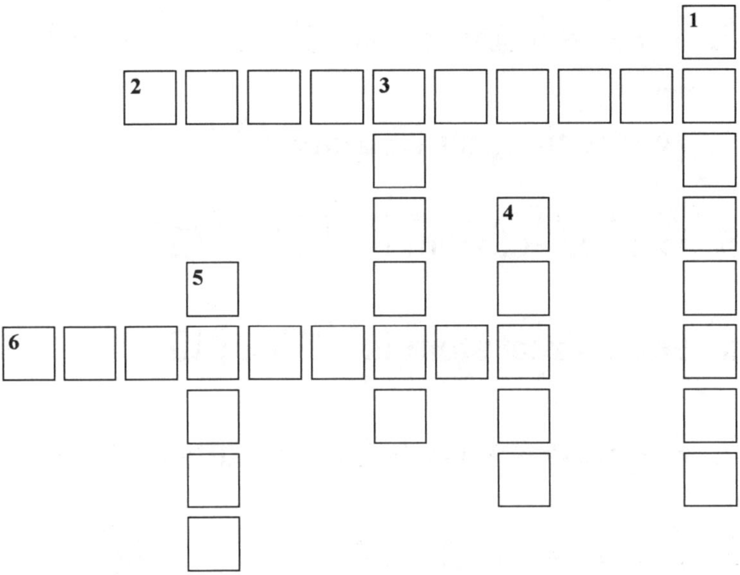

Clues

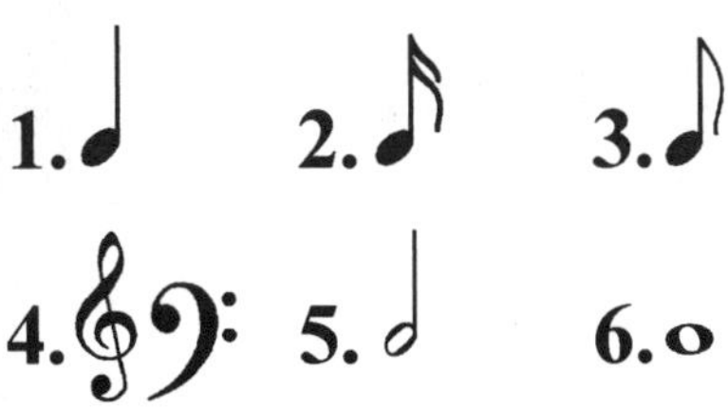

Multiple Choice 2

Tick ☑ the correct answer.

1. This note 𝅗𝅥 is a crotchet ☐ minim ☐

2. ♪ × 2 = a crotchet ☐ minim ☐

3. 𝅗𝅥 + 𝅗𝅥 = a semibreve ☐ semiquaver ☐

4. 𝅘𝅥𝅯𝅘𝅥𝅯 = a crotchet ☐ quaver ☐

5. The correct stem is ☐ ☐

6. The correct stem is ☐ ☐

7. ♩. = three quavers ☐ four quavers ☐

8. ♩ ♩ ♩ = 𝅗𝅥 ☐ 𝅗𝅥. ☐

9. ♩. + ♪ = 𝅗𝅥 ☐ 𝅝 ☐

10. ♩♪ (tied) = ♩. ☐ 𝅗𝅥 ☐

A Mystery Word

My first letter is in **charm** ☐
But isn't in **chair**.
My second is in **pure** ☐
But not in **pear**.
My third is in **shop** ☐
But isn't in **hope**.
My fourth is in **ripe** ☐
But not in **rope**.
My fifth is in **care** ☐
But not in **dear**.

The letters spell something
We all like to hear.
Write your answer here _ _ _ _ _

Match Each Note and Rest

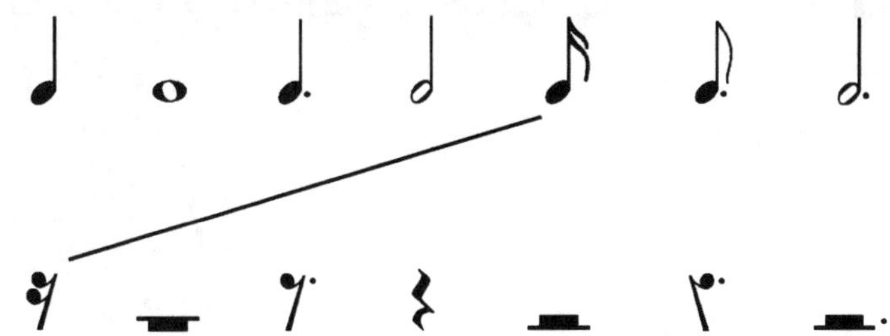

Remember
SnooZe
for a Crotchet

☐ / 7

Musical Matchword

Use a different colour for each word.

MIN	SS
CRO	BLE
SH	NE
QUA	**IM**
TRE	RAL
SE	TCHET
NATU	QUAVER
FL	MIBREVE
SEMI	AT
BA	VER
SEMIT	ARP
TO	ONE

/12

Merry-Go-Round

The last letter of each word is also used to start the next word. Follow the merry-go-round to find the answers.

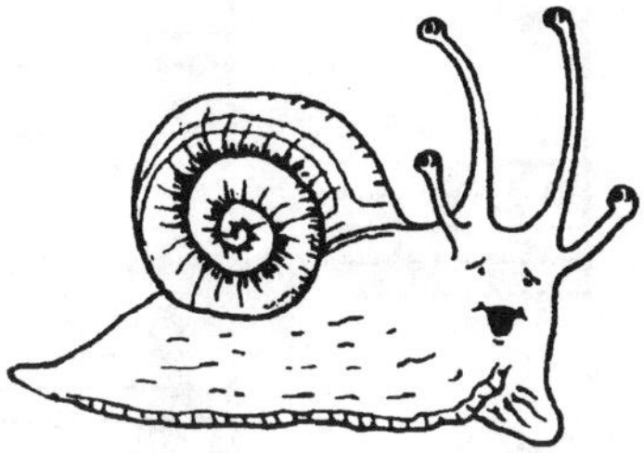

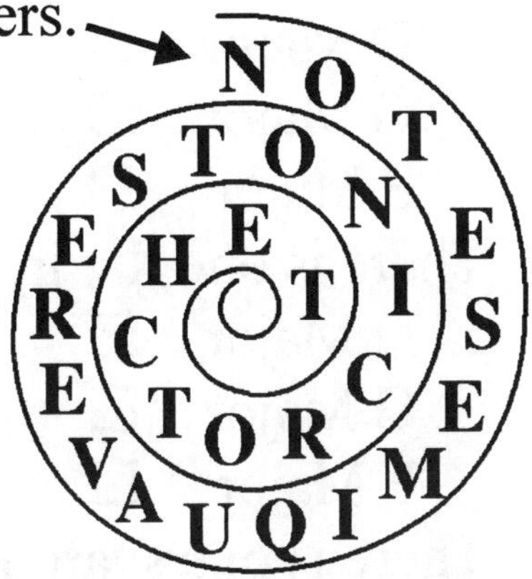

Clues:

1. You need these to write music _ _ _ _ _

2. Four of these equal one crotchet _ _ _ _ _ _ _ _ _ _

3. This is when notes are not played _ _ _ _

4. This is the first note of a scale _ _ _ _ _

5. Four of these equal one semibreve _ _ _ _ _ _ _ _

/ **5**

Multiple Choice 3

Tick ☑ the correct answer

1. There are 2 sharps in
   - D Major ☐
   - G Major ☐
   - F Major ☐

2. There is one flat in
   - D Major ☐
   - G Major ☐
   - F Major ☐

3. There is one sharp in
   - D Major ☐
   - G Major ☐
   - F Major ☐

4. In Major Scales there is one semitone
   - between notes 2-3 and notes 6-7 ☐
   - between notes 3-4 and notes 7-8 ☐
   - between notes 4-5 and notes 7-8 ☐
5. An Octave is the
   - 4th degree of the scale ☐
   - 7th degree of the scale ☐
   - 8th degree of the scale ☐

/5

Multiple choice 4

Tick ☑ the correct answer

1. A Tonic Triad has
   - 5 notes ☐
   - 3 notes ☐
2. A Melodic Interval has two notes written
   - one after the other ☐
   - one above the other ☐
3. In a Melodic Interval the notes are played
   - at the same time ☐
   - separately ☐
4. In a Harmonic Interval the notes are written
   - one after the other ☐
   - one above the other ☐
5. In a Harmonic Interval the notes are played
   - at the same time ☐
   - separately ☐

/5

A Number Crossword

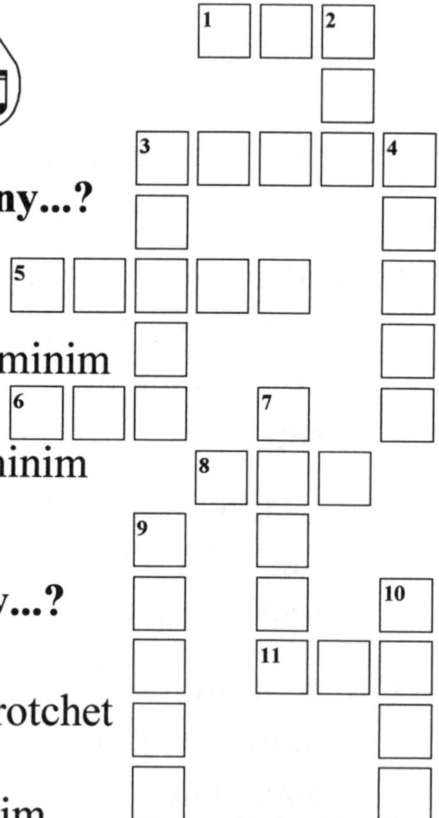

Clues Across: How many...?

1. Sharps in D Major
3. Notes in a tonic triad
5. Crotchets in a dotted minim
6. Sharps in G Major
8. Quavers in a dotted minim
11. Semitones in a tone

Clues Down: How many...?

2. Flats in F Major
3. Quavers in a dotted crotchet
4. Notes in an octave
7. Semiquavers in a minim
9. Letter names of notes are there
10. Crotchets in a semibreve

12

Tick or Cross

Tick ☑ if correct, cross ☒ if not correct.

1. $\frac{2}{4}$ = two quaver beats in a bar. ☐
2. $\frac{3}{4}$ = three crotchet beats in a bar. ☐
3. $\frac{4}{4}$ = four crotchet beats in a bar. ☐
4. $\frac{2}{4}$ = two crotchet beats in a bar. ☐
5. $\frac{2}{4}$ = Simple Quadruple Time. ☐
6. $\frac{3}{4}$ = Simple Triple Time. ☐
7. $\frac{2}{4}$ = Simple Duple Time. ☐
8. $\frac{4}{4}$ = Simple Quadruple Time. ☐
9. In time signatures the bottom number tells you what kind of beats in a bar. ☐
10. In time signatures the top number tells you how many beats in a bar. ☐

/10

Look for the Terms

① Play the music at a moderate speed

allegretto	slightly slower than allegro
andante	at a walking pace
moderato	at a moderate pace

Match and colour the parts of each word.

AND	ATO
MODER	ANTE
ALLEG	RETTO

/ 3

② Play the music loudly or softly.

piano (*p*)	soft
pianissimo (*pp*)	very soft
forte (*f*)	loud
fortissimo (*ff*)	very loud

Match and colour the parts of each word.

PI	ISSIMO
FORTI	E
PIAN	ANO
FORT	SSIMO

/ 4

Look for the Terms

3 Play the music slowly

lento	slowly
adagio	slow, leisurely
largo	slow, stately, broad

Find each word in the letters below. Use a different colour for each word.

A L D A L G E I

A O R G N O T O

3

4 Play the music quickly

allegro	lively, reasonably fast
vivace	lively, quick
presto	very quick
prestissimo	as fast as possible

Find the four musical terms.

Z P A D B V U V T I Z
P R E S T I S S I M O
S E B U K V N H W P Y
G S L T O A N Q U A R
X T V H U C E L E G R
B O A L L E G R O A N

4

Match the Words and Meanings

Put the correct **letter** in the correct box.

1 adagio

2 >

3 allegro

4 

5 prestissimo

6 

7 allegretto

8 

9 presto

10 lento

11 

12 largo

A slightly slower than allegro

B lively, reasonably fast

C becoming softer

D very quick

E slowly

F slow, leisurely

G accent the note

H becoming louder

I pause on the note

J as fast as possible

K slow and stately, broad

L staccato [short, detached]

1	2	3	4	5	6	7	8	9	10	11	12
F											

/12

Musical Terms Crossword

Clues Across

1. Lively, Quick
4. Hold back, slower at once
5. At a walking pace
6. A little slower or a little faster than andante
9. Speed, time
10. Soft

Clues Down

2. In a singing style
3. At a moderate pace
7. Sweetly
8. A little

Is it TWO or is it THREE?

Ask someone to play a short piece of music for you with **two** beats in a bar. Listen to it carefully.

Now ask them to play it again. This time **tap** the beats, making the first beat stronger than the second beat... **one** two, **one** two. Clap your hands... **one** two, **one** two... stamp your feet... **one** two, **one** two... bang a drum...**one** two, **one** two... or.... well, I'm sure you can think of some other ways!

Question: In **two beat time**, is the first or the second beat of the bar the strong beat?
Answer: ________________________________

When you are sure about tapping two beats in a bar, listen to some music that has **three** beats in a bar. The strong beat is still the first beat in each bar but you have to count **one**, two, three this time. Clap your hands... **one** , two, three... stamp your foot... **one**, two, three... beat your drum or perhaps two pieces of wood... **one**, two, three... **one**, two, three.

Question: In **three beat time** which beat is the strong beat?
Answer: ________________________________

When you are really good at tapping the beats, ask for the music to be played with **either** two beats **or** three beats in a bar.

Spot the Difference

Here are two bars of music.

Version 1 

Here are two more bars of music. They look almost the same but they are not exactly the same.

Version 2 

Clap each set of two bars. Can you spot the difference? The answer is at the bottom of the page.

Make up your own 'trick question'. Write two lots of two-bar music with slightly different rhythms. Play them to Mum or Dad and see if they can 'spot the difference'.

Version 1 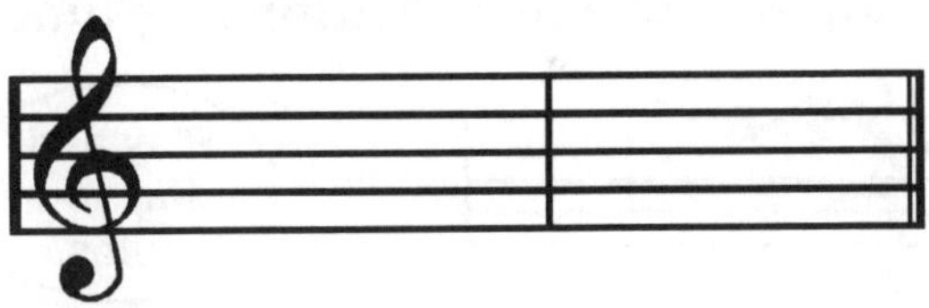

Version 2 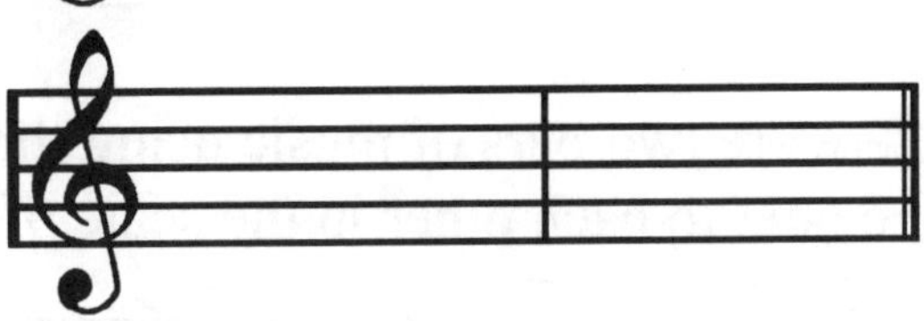

Try others in 2, 3 or 4 beat time.

The second bar has a dotted note (a dotted crotchet) in version 1.

Echoes

Play these three notes on your instrument. They are next to each other in the scale of **C Major**.

Here are three notes next to each other from the scale of **F Major** in $\frac{3}{4}$ time.

Now you write one bar of music using three notes from the scale of **G Major** in $\frac{2}{4}$ time.

Here are two bars of music using three notes that are next to each other in the scale of **D Major**.

If you sing them correctly you will sound like an echo.

Now you can write some more two bar tunes. They must have only three notes that are next to each other in the scale. Play them and then sing them.

1. In the key of C Major

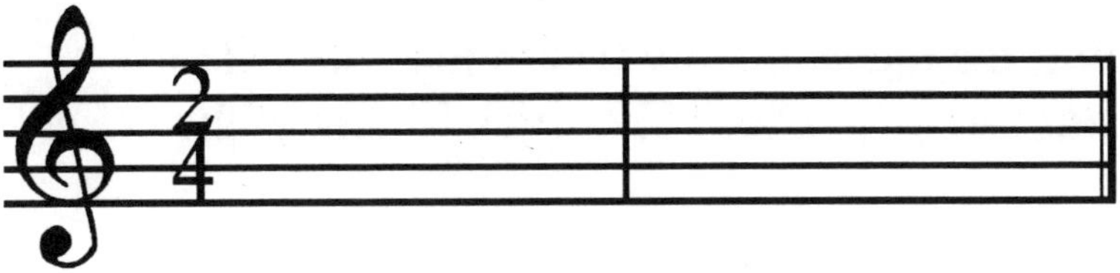

2. In the key of ___ Major

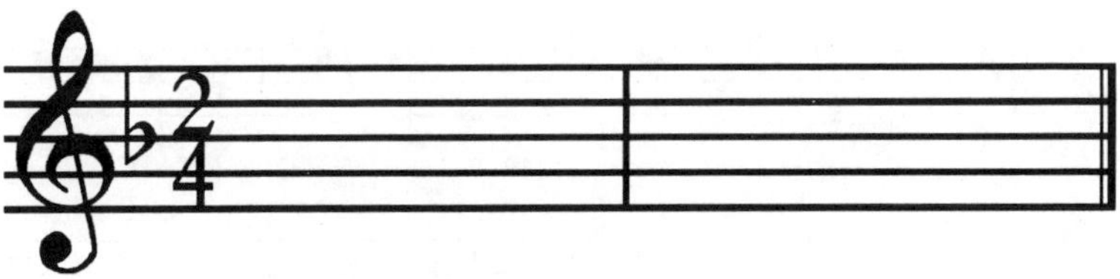

3. In the key of ___ Major

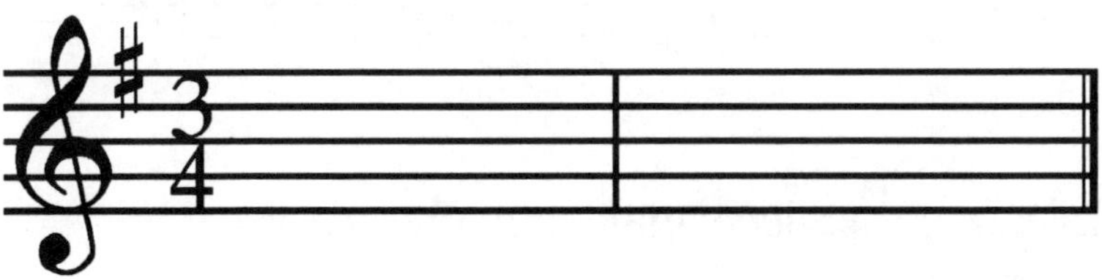

4. In the key of ___ Major

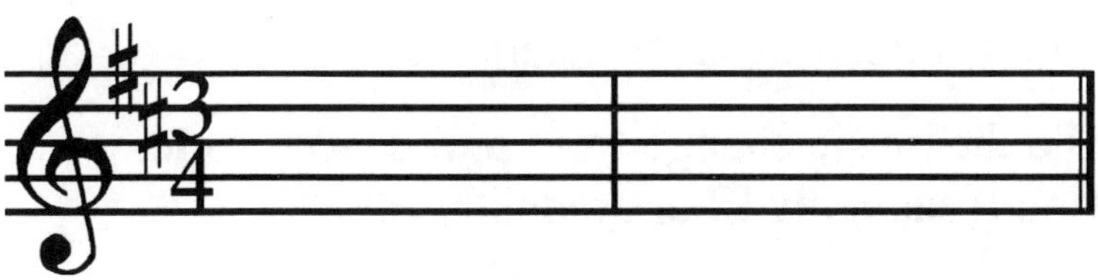

Listen Carefully

forte (loud) or **piano** (soft)?
Ask someone to play the music on this page.
Afterwards try to answer this question.

1. Was the music mainly **legato** (smooth) ☐ or **staccato** (detached) ☐? [tick ☑ **one** of the boxes]

Listen to the piece again and afterwards try to answer these questions.

2. Did the music begin loudly ☐ or quietly ☐?

3. Did it end loudly ☐ or quietly ☐?

4. Did the music change from **piano** (soft) to **forte** (loud) suddenly ☐ or gradually ☐?